Maisie
and the
Nantucket Daffodil Parade

by Bretworth Barry Apthorp

Illustrations by Ros Webb

I dedicate this book to:

My husband, Ken, for without his countless hours of mechanic work, Maisie would still be rotting away in Western Massachusetts.

My children, Greyson, Hilary and Nate, and my grandson, Josiah, for teaching me of the love in a child's eye when a story is read aloud.

My father, for giving Maisie to me and suggesting that she come live in Nantucket with me.

Once upon a time, in a far off corner of Western Massachusetts, lived a very sad old car. Her owner had fallen on hard times and could no longer keep the old car running so he pushed her into an ancient red barn and shut the door. "Where am I? What is this place?" asked the old car. The barn was filled to the brim with antique farm equipment, bales of hay and the memories of a once prosperous farm.

Days turned into weeks, which turned into years. "I have been here for 18 long and lonely years," sighed the old car, "I am getting older, rustier and sadder by the day." She stared through the slats of light in the barn door to the sunshine outside and dreamed of driving down the winding country roads, her top down, her wheels spinning and a glimpse of a smile on her grille. "Oh, if only I could," she thought.

One morning there was a clink and a clank at the barn doors. "What could that be?" thought the old car. No one had entered the barn in many years. The door creaked open and in came a woman with a man who had a funny accent. They came up to the old car and opened the doors, the hood and the trunk. They poked this and jiggled that, turned knobs and pulled levers. "The car is for you," said the man with the accent, "I think she would be perfect for Nantucket Island." "Nantucket Island?" thought the old car. "No red barn, rusty farm equipment or musty bales of hay?" So many thoughts were racing through the old car's mind – she was overjoyed that she would finally be leaving the old red barn.

The next morning the woman came back with a different man, who was tall and strong and looked as though he could handle anything. The woman opened the car door and sat in the driver's seat, behind the large round steering wheel. "This is the most beautiful little car," the woman said. "She seems like a prim and proper lady, and I think I shall call her 'Maisie'. " "Maisie?" exclaimed the old car, "Yes, I like that. I think that 'Maisie' will be a great name for me."

That day was spent pulling Maisie out of the barn and towing her all the way to the beautiful blue ocean and the ferry that would sail her to Nantucket Island. "The air is so fresh, the sun so bright and the water so blue," thought Maisie, "I am very grateful to be out in the open and on an adventure." She creaked and moaned all the way to the ferry and felt every one of the 18 years that she sat unmoving in the old red barn.

The ferry eventually sailed off and reached the island. The dock was filled with many other old cars. "This must be the place for old cars to go," thought Maisie, "but these other cars are not dull and dented like me. In fact, they have no dents at all. Their chrome gleams, their paint sparkles, and they don't have rips in their seats."

The fancy cars were talking excitedly amongst themselves about something called the Daffodil Parade. By listening, Maisie learned that this is a parade held on the island for beautiful antique cars that have been decorated with vibrant yellow daffodils. "This parade sounds like such fun," exclaimed Maisie to the beautiful cars, "I can't wait to be a part of it!"

"You???" said the fancy purple car with a silver pinstripe, "You have dents, rust, rips and holes. You don't even run! You aren't like us at all! How could you possibly be good enough, or pretty enough, to be in the Daffodil Parade?"

Maisie was embarrassed. She didn't realize that you had to be beautiful to have fun, and besides, the woman said that she was the most beautiful little car in the world. Didn't she? Maisie felt very sad and confused.

The fancy antique cars drove off, their engines purring, to join the Daffodil Parade. Maisie was towed off the dock to her new home with the woman and the tall man.

Over the next year the tall man worked on Maisie's engine, and when he turned the key, she roared to life! "What a wonderful sound," the woman cried, "I knew you could fix her," she said to the tall man. Maisie was so happy! "Maybe I will drive down that long and winding country road after all," she thought. That afternoon, and many afternoons afterward, the woman and the tall man took Maisie for a drive down the long and winding Polpis Road, with her top down, her wheels spinning. "This is the life," sighed Maisie happily.

It was April, and the talk of Nantucket town was the Daffodil Parade. Daffodils lined all the streets in a fantastic celebration of yellow. The woman was preparing what she would make for the picnic basket, and the tall man was putting a final coat of wax on Maisie, buffing the dullness out of her paint and propping up her seats with a block of wood. "Oh how lovely," smiled Maisie, as the woman tied gorgeous bouquets of daffodils together with colorful ribbons and bows, draping them over Maisie's hood and trunk. "I feel very beautiful, and I am ready to face the mean antique cars who said I wasn't pretty enough or good enough to join the parade!!"

As she drove up Main Street, she could see the fancy cars lining up to join the parade. She pulled up behind the purple car with the silver pinstripe that she had met the year before at the ferry. "You again?" snarled the purple car, "What are you doing here? To make us laugh? Surely it isn't because you are beautiful or one of us!"

"I am here because I want to have fun, and you don't have to be beautiful to have that. My owners love me and think I am the best little car in the world. I may be dented and rusty and have rips in my seats, but I bring smiles to people's faces wherever I go," said Maisie. "We can't all be beautiful like you, but we can all have a positive attitude and enjoy the gift of life that has been given to us – and that is what I intend to do!"

This is how Maisie came to be a part of the Daffodil Parade. Covered in golden daffodils, ribbons and bows, she chugged out to 'Sconset village, honking her horn and flashing her lights. Forgotten were the lonely days of being neglected in the old red barn, forgotten were the insults given by the fancy cars. "I am in the Daffodil Parade. I am loved. I am happy," laughed Maisie. This happiness showed in every dent, rip and wrinkle, and because of that, she was the most beautiful car in the parade. The crowds shouted as she passed "We love you, Maisie," and everyone wanted to take her picture. Even the purple car with the silver pinstripe was impressed and humbled by the attention that she was getting!

Every year in April, you will find Maisie and her owners, happily chugging through the streets of Nantucket Island in the Daffodil Parade – dents, rips, squeaks, rust and all. If you look very closely you might even see a glimpse of a smile in Maisie's grille!

 Bretworth Barry Apthorp lives on Nantucket Island with her husband, Ken, two Chihuahuas and, of course, Maisie. When she is not driving around in Maisie, she can be found in her studio making fine silver jewelry inspired by the beauty around her. She loves walking on the beach, gardening and spending time with her family. You can see her handmade jewelry at www.twoforjoyjewelry.com.

 Ros Webb studied fashion and design and became a fashion designer before pursuing a career illustrating and writing children's books. She has been illustrating children's books for close to a decade and developed her own style as a children book artist following the birth of her first daughter and the publication of her picture book "The Big Sleepy Bear and the Pink Flamingos." Ros lives in the Irish mountains and is greatly inspired by her three children, fours dogs and four cats. She has worked extensively with authors from across the globe and is continually inspired by their imagination and story telling.

CPSIA information can be obtained at www.ICGtesting.com
Printed in the USA
BVIW12n0515120417
480870BV00001B/1